Stamps

R. F. SCHOOLLEY-WEST

The British Library

Published by
The British Library
Great Russell Street
London
WC1B 3DG

and 27 South Main Street
Wolfeboro, New Hampshire
03894–2069

British Library Cataloguing in
Publication Data

Schoolley-West, R. F.
Stamps.
1. Postage stamps—Collectors
and collecting
I. Title II. British Library
769.56′075 HE6213

ISBN 0-7123-0127-5

Library of Congress Catalog
Card No. 87-27732.

Designed by Roger Davies
Typeset in Monophoto Ehrhardt
by August Filmsetting, Haydock,
St Helens
Colour origination by York
House Graphics, Hanwell
Printed in England by
Jolly and Barber Ltd, Rugby

Contents

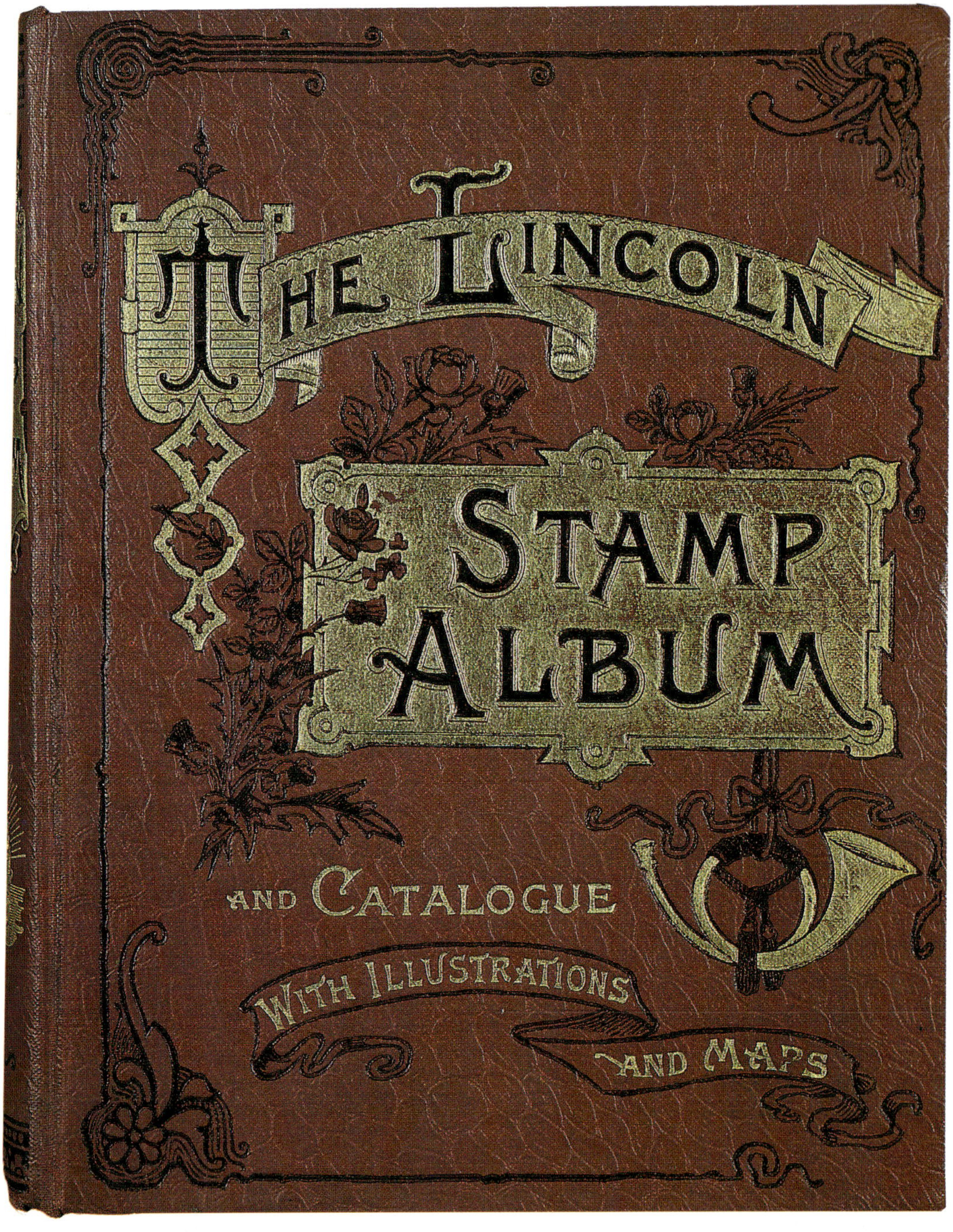

1 A nineteenth-century collector's album.

Introduction

Early postal services

A form of postal system was operated by the Egyptians about 4,000 years ago which involved couriers travelling by whatever means of transport was available, and it is known that between 2,000 and 2,500 years ago, both the Chinese and the Persians had systems involving stage horses as the means of transport. The development of the great civilisations of Greece and Rome saw the introduction of postal courier systems, the messages being transmitted on wax or clay tablets. In medieval times, itinerant traders no doubt provided an informal postal service.

The Royal Mails

In England, the first organised 'Royal Mail', using couriers, was set up by King John in the twelfth century. King Henry VIII refined the Royal Mail system by employing post horses and appointed Sir Robert Tuke as his Postmaster; but it was not until Queen Elizabeth I instituted regulations to control the conveyance of mail that the system, as it is known in the United Kingdom today, began to evolve.

In the fifteenth century, a royal mail service operated in France which, subject to censorship and the payment of substantial fees, the public were allowed to use. During the same century the sophisticated and extensive service of the Counts of Thurn and Taxis was set up – and such was its success and efficiency that it survived for more than four hundred years until being taken over by Prussia in 1867.

Such systems prevailed until the seventeenth century, with increasing refinement and access granted to the general public; generally they were operated not on any accepted official national basis, but rather according to the requirements of the commercial world and the seats of learning – the monasteries and universities. In England, the first royal consent to a private letter service was given in 1635 to Thomas Witherings, and this operated on a number of strictly limited routes from London. After the English Civil War, a postal act was passed by Parliament which established the State's monopoly of postal services, and appointed specific charges.

The first adhesive stamps

Whilst the establishment of postal charges was a significant development in the operation of a public service, they were often difficult to calculate and could cause delays. What is more, such was the level of many of the charges that the services were often beyond the pocket of many of the public. It was this situation that resulted in Rowland Hill (2) examining the workings of the Post Office, culminating in the publication of his pamphlet *Post Office Reform* in 1837. He detailed the difficulties of the existing system and put forward the case for a prepaid uniform rate of charge by weight.

Eventually Hill's suggestions were accepted by Parliament and on 10 January 1840 uniform Penny Postage was introduced.

The efficient operation of a prepaid system required some means of satisfactory accounting for the fees paid and it needed to be clear that letters had indeed been prepaid; to this end, in September 1839, the Treasury announced a competition to obtain suitable designs for letter sheets and stamps for the purpose. It was from this competition that the cover and wrapper designs of William Mulready (4) and the basis of a design for an adhesive postage stamp by Rowland Hill were adopted, the latter resulting in the introduction of the world's first adhesive postage stamp, the Penny Black, for use from 6 May 1840.

The envelope design of Mulready was subjected to considerable criticism, to such an extent that it was withdrawn in 1841, leaving the adhesive stamps of Hill as the principal means of operating the prepaid service. Such was their success that it was inevitable that other countries would adopt a similar system.

Stamp collecting

As with other art forms, the 'new' stamps were clear candidates for collectors and it is highly likely that they were collected from the outset (1); this interest has never waned and the hobby of stamp collecting is arguably the most widely pursued pastime in the world.

The subject of philately represents the serious side of this hobby, being the study of a very wide range of aspects of the history of the posts, design, printing and a host of other areas related to this important field of human communications and history. In very many countries the postal services are recognised as an important part of the country's commercial and social development; not only is it ensured that specific events are incorporated in the design of commemorative stamps but, more importantly perhaps, public collections are maintained. Postal museums are usually run by postal administrations out of pride in their history. However, other institutions such as libraries, national museums and societies have also established their own collections, generally in a less restricted way than those of the postal administration.

The British Museum was no exception to this. It has been suggested that as early as the 1860s proposals were made to the Trustees by Dr John Gray (3), the then Keeper of Zoology, and Mr William Vaux, Keeper of Coins and Medals, that a national collection of postage stamps should be formed at the Museum.

2 Sir Rowland Hill.

3 Dr John Gray.

The Foundations of the Philatelic Collections

It was not until 1891 that the suggestion of Gray and Vaux became a reality with the bequest of the collection of Thomas Keay Tapling, MP. Although the collections were not established at the instigation of Gray, he nevertheless left his mark on philately, for he was an enthusiastic collector and writer on the subject. That he commenced his collecting in 1840 by purchasing penny blacks may be the subject of considerable doubt, but his published works, in particular his series of articles entitled 'Postage Stamps of the World' which appeared in the *Young England* magazine (brought together in December 1862 and published as *A Hand Catalogue of Postage Stamps for the use of Collectors*) makes him one of the earliest philatelic authors; his works are today to be found in the printed book collections in the British Library.

From the establishment of the Museum's Philatelic Collections, they have grown to realise the ambitions of Gray and Vaux by the addition of gifts and bequests during the intervening years, and now represent a formidable gathering of philatelic collections and

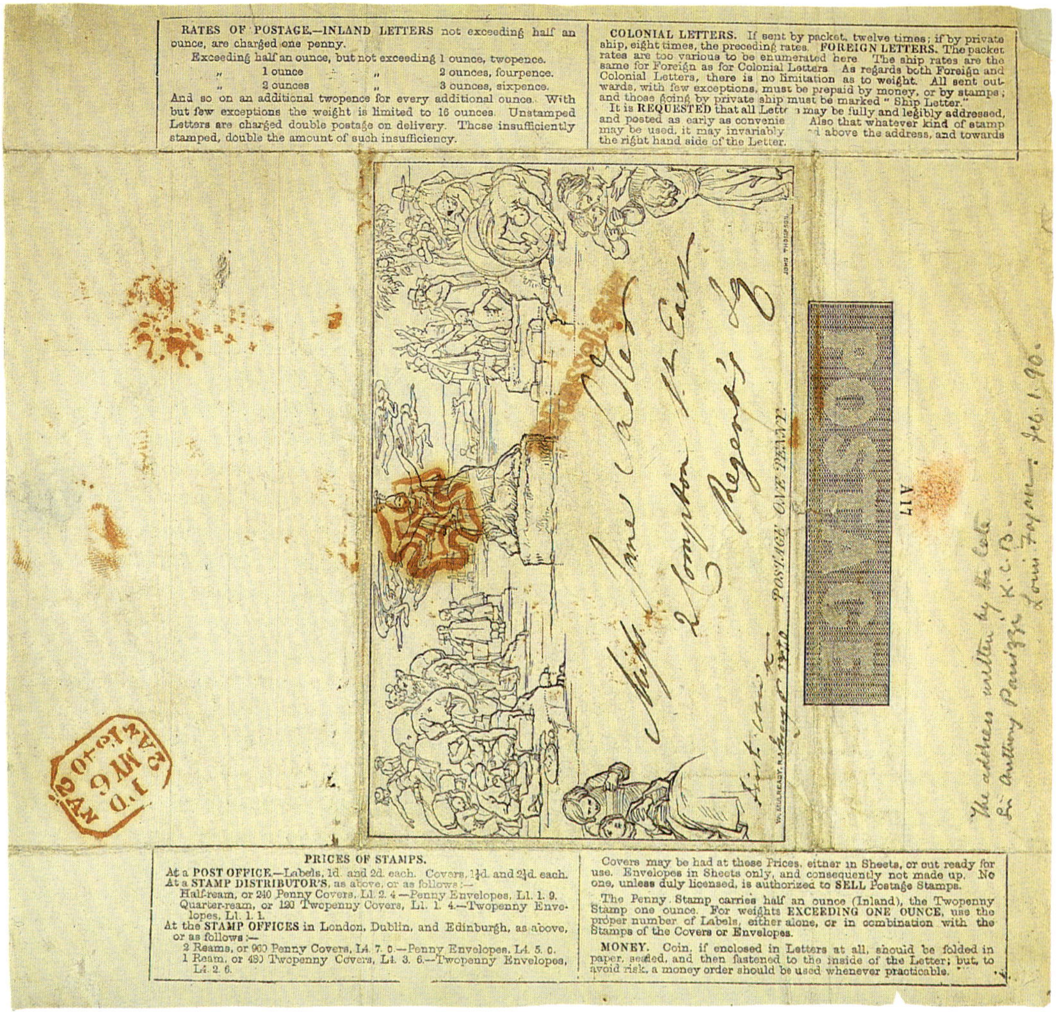

4 A Mulready lettersheet posted on 6 May 1840.

material, to the extent that they stand on equal terms alongside all the other great national collections. Indeed, the range of subjects and the volume of material maintained make them arguably the finest collections of philatelic material in the world. Supported by large collections of literature, maps, official publications, newspapers and manuscripts, the British Library is the only institution anywhere to offer philatelic researchers such a comprehensive service.

The following chapters aim to give an insight into the collections and a background to some of the rare and interesting items to be found within them.

The Tapling Collection

Top. 1843 United States. Baltimore, Md. Postmaster's provisional used on cover.

Centre. Steinmeyer's City Post, Oakland, S. Carolina.

Bottom. Mexico 1856. Stamp from Chihuahua District Office.

5 Thomas Keay Tapling, MP.

6 Edward Denny Bacon.

Thomas Tapling

The foundation of Britain's National Philatelic Collections came as a result of the bequest of Thomas Keay Tapling, MP (5) of his collections of postage and telegraph stamps and postal stationery. The collection ranked among the finest in the nineteenth century and today stands alone as being the only one of those famous collections to remain intact.

Thomas Keay Tapling was born on 30 October 1855, and at the age of 15 years went to Harrow School; from there he went up to Trinity College Cambridge, obtaining his BA and LL.B degrees in 1880 and MA and LL.M in 1883. After initially studying medicine, in 1880 he was called to the Bar at the Inner Temple and on his father's death in 1882 he took over as the head of the family's large carpet manufacturing and marketing firm, Thomas Tapling & Company. Tapling was clearly a person of considerable influence with an interest in politics. In the 1885 General Election he was defeated as the Conservative candidate in the Harborough Division of Leicestershire; however, just one year later he contested the same seat again and was elected with a substantial majority.

Tapling is believed to have started to collect stamps when he was 10 years old, and is believed to have joined the Philatelic Society, London (later the Royal Philatelic Society, London) at about the age of 15 years. In 1881 he was elected vice-president, an office which he held until his untimely death at the age of 35 years on 11 April 1891.

In spite of his short life, Tapling assembled a formidable collection which, in terms of content, is today unsurpassed. It covers the issues of the whole world from 1840 to approximately 1890 and, as well as the basic issues, includes virtually all the major rarities together with essays, proofs, colour trials, and errors, most of which today are still of superb fresh colour. When viewing the Tapling Collection, it must be borne in mind that it is still an original Victorian collection which displays the captioning style of the time. These captions were however prepared to the highest standard of knowledge available then, by E. D. Bacon.

Edward Bacon

Edward Denny Bacon (later Sir Edward Bacon) (6) was the person the Trustees of the British Museum engaged in 1891 to carry out the huge task of arranging and captioning the Tapling Collection – a task accomplished by Bacon during the next eight years with the assistance of Miss Jane Hamilton. Bacon was a close friend of Tapling and was a man with a profound philatelic knowledge; he could be considered the greatest philatelic researcher of all time, much of his published work still representing the standard information available today. He was also very active in the Philatelic Society,

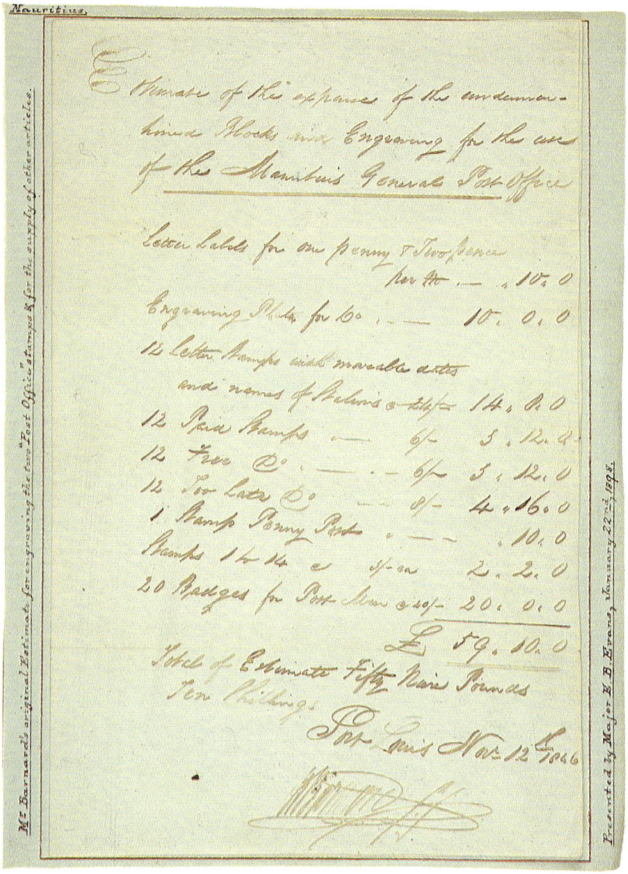

Mauritius.

Mr Barnard's original Estimate for engraving the two "Post Office" stamps &c for the supply of other articles.

Estimate of the expense of the undermentioned Blocks and Engraving for the use of the Mauritius General Post Office

Letter Labels for one penny & Twopence per 100 — . 10. 0
Engraving Plate for Do . — 10. 0. 0
12 Letter Stamps with moveable dates and names of Stations @ — 14. 0. 0
12 Paid Stamps — 6/- 3. 12. 0
12 Free Do — 6/- 3. 12. 0
12 Too Late Do — 8/- 4. 16. 0
1 Stamp Penny Post . — . 10. 0
Stamps 1 to 14 @ 3/- 2. 2. 0
20 Badges for Post Men @ 20/- 20. 0. 0
£ 59. 10. 0

Total of Estimate Fifty Nine Pounds Ten Shillings

Port Louis Nov 12th 1846

Presented by Major E. B. Evans, January 22nd 1898.

7 Barnard's estimate for producing the first issues of Mauritius.

8 Mauritius 1847 2d 'Post Office'.

London, serving as Treasurer, Secretary, and Vice-President, until eventually being elected President of the Society in 1917. Bacon was a member of the Expert Committee of the Society from its inception in 1883 and was a close friend and adviser to many of the principal collectors of his day, notably the Earl of Crawford, whose philatelic library he classified and catalogued, and also Henry J. Duveen and King George V, who appointed him his curator in 1913 upon the death of J. A. Tilleard, an office he held until his death in 1938.

The 'Post Office' Mauritius

The Tapling Collection comprises approximately 100,000 items and it is difficult to select just a few for special mention. However, with all the outstanding items that there are, some still stand in a class of their own, not the least of which are the famous 'Post Office' issues of Mauritius. There are many who, whilst they are not collectors, will still have heard of these exceedingly rare items which take only second place to the 1856 1 cent magenta of British Guiana, of which only one item has ever been found.

9 Trinidad 1847 *Lady McLeod.*

In 1847 the Island of Mauritius issued its first postage stamps. An estimate for the design and engraving of the stamps, together with the production of a number of other items which were required by the Post Office, was sought from a local engraver and printer, Joseph Barnard (7). Just 500 of each of the 1d and 2d denominations were produced, of which very few examples of the 1d and even less of the 2d have been found, with only four of the latter being known in unused condition. Whilst these items are rare, and merit their famous status on that basis alone, their fame has been enhanced by myths perpetuated relating to their production and usage, namely that they were erroneously inscribed 'Post Office' (8); that Barnard was an old, partially sighted jeweller and watchmaker and that the stamps resulted from an idea promoted by Lady Gomm, the wife of the Governor of Mauritius. That the inscription on the stamps was a mistake is belied by the fact that this form of wording had been in use on cancellers since the 1820s, and that the new adhesive stamps merely continued the traditional form until it was changed on the second issue which appeared in May 1848. It is a matter of fact that Barnard is recorded as an engraver and miniature painter, with no evidence that he operated as a jewel-

ler or watchmaker, and when one examines the quality of the engraving of the stamps, which were done whilst he was in his thirties, it is clearly a gross distortion of the truth to suggest that he was either partially-sighted or old. It is true that some of the stamps were used on invitations (see **back cover**) to a Ball which was held at Government House, and that there are some indications that a first printing might have been carried out to make them available quickly for that purpose; however, that this was all done very quickly for Lady Gomm's benefit cannot be supported. The fact remains that these items are as rare and as popular as they always have been.

Early adhesives

In 1843, prior to the Mauritius stamp issue, the Swiss canton of Zurich produced two stamps to prepay local postage and that to the neighbouring cantons; the denominations issued were 4 rappen (**10**) and 6 rappen. Both of these stamps are rare and were printed from five different transfer types which can be seen in horizontal strips; multiples showing the types are extremely rare and the strips in the Tapling Collection are amongst the largest known pieces.

It is not surprising that some of the early adhesive postage stamps were produced for local or specific use; such was the case with the first stamp of Trinidad which was issued for private local use on 24 April 1847. For some time the postal services in Trinidad had been haphazard, and the owners of a steamship, the *Lady McLeod*, saw the opportunity to generate additional business for the vessel, which regularly sailed between San Fernando and Port of Spain. These ports were also the principal route for mail and it represented little extra work to provide a postal service via the ship. A stamp was produced which, whilst bearing no denomination, was sold at five

10 Zurich 1843 4 rappen.

cents apiece or discounted at the rate of four dollars per hundred; each letter was required to carry one of the stamps as evidence of prepayment and, on receipt of a letter, the stamp was usually cancelled with pen and ink by the Captain to prevent re-use (9).

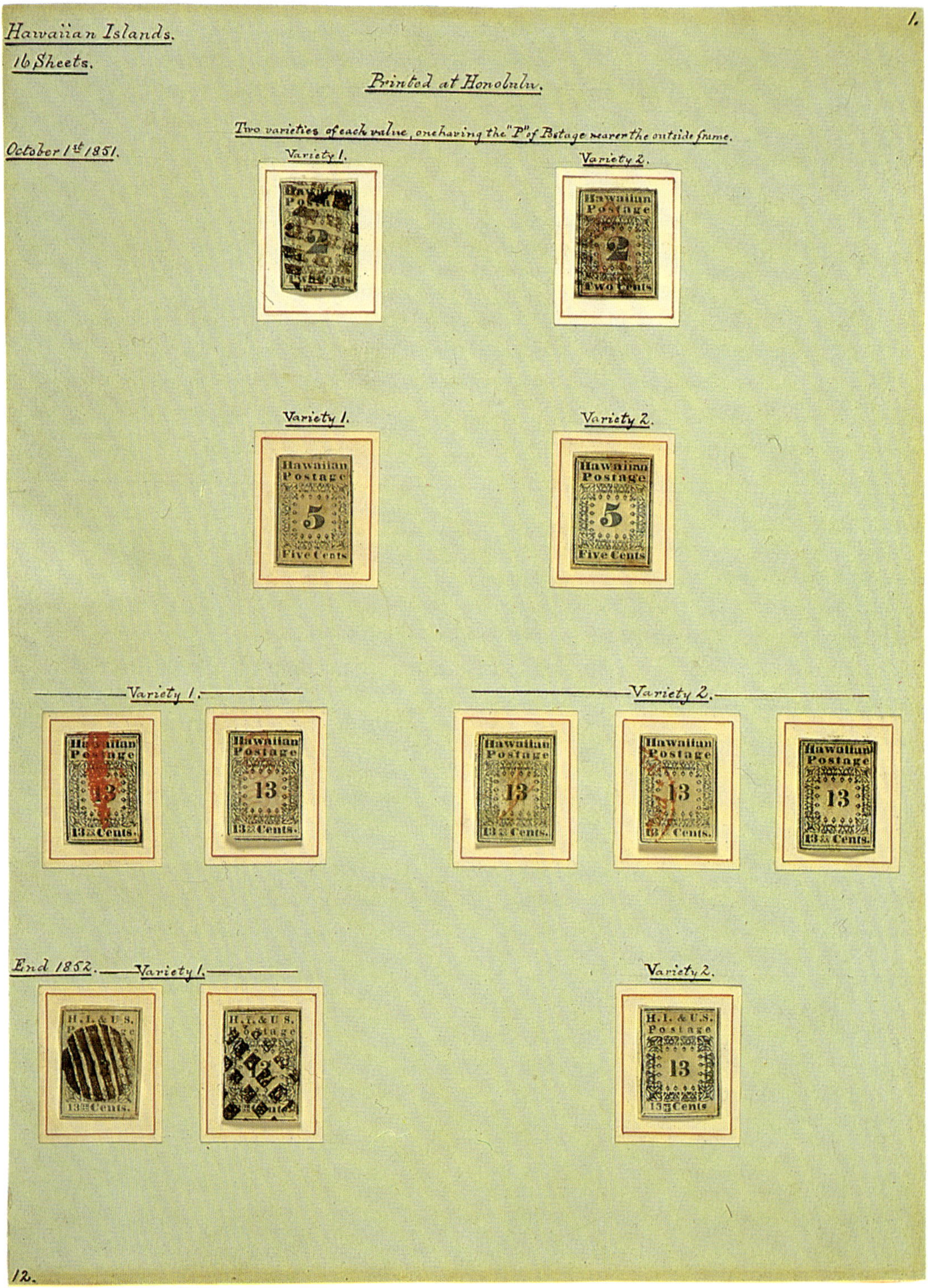
Hawaiian Islands.
16 Sheets.
1.
Printed at Honolulu.
Two varieties of each value, one having the "P" of Postage nearer the outside frame.
October 1st 1851.
Variety 1.
Variety 2.
Variety 1.
Variety 2.
Variety 1.
Variety 2.
End 1852.
Variety 1.
Variety 2.
12.

11 *opposite*. Hawaiian 'Missionaries'.

12 *top*. British Guiana 1850–51 4 cents on lemon-yellow.

13 *centre left*. Gold Coast 1883 1d surcharge on 4d.

14 *centre right*. India 1854 4 annas – inverted head.

15 *left*. Western Australia 1854 4d – inverted frame.

The Gold Coast rarity

'Uniqueness' is not a word that is really valid in philately for, even today, new finds still occur; more correctly, items exist which are the only ones known. In the British Library's collection there are a number of examples in this category, the most well-known being found in the Gold Coast section, the 1883 1d surcharge on 4d (13). Tapling acquired the item from Bacon, who had purchased it from a dealer in London. That there was a shortage of 1d stamps in the Gold Coast in May 1883, when this item is believed to have been issued, is well recorded. However, there are no official records or local references to the issue of this provisional surcharge and, in the absence of positive evidence, its status will always be in question. Only one other item has been seen, and that was declared to be a forgery in 1947; although another similar one was reported to be in a famous Parisian collection in the early part of the century, it has never been reported by anyone as having been seen, nor has it ever come to light.

'Missionaries' and 'Cottonreels'

Assessment of status is always a problem in the case of extremely rare items, for it is necessary to be able to compare them with authenticated genuine material; this criterion can be fulfilled when a few genuinely used items exist and they are supported by the existence of official or other records. Such is the case with the Hawaiian issues of 1851. Known as 'Missionaries' because the majority of them were used by missionaries in Honolulu, they are among the great rarities of the world. Three values were issued of 2, 5 and 13 cents and of these the 2 cents is the rarest, with only fifteen examples known to have survived, two of them being in the collection. The page illustrated (11) represents approximately 10 per cent of all known examples. The stamps were printed on thin, hard paper; it is certainly the main reason why they did not survive, and why those that have are mostly damaged. There is a reasonably well-authenticated story associated with one of the 2 cent stamps, that a collector murdered another to acquire the item for his own collection; the incident took place in Paris at the end of the last century when a well-known collector was found murdered and, whilst there were items of considerable value in his flat, nothing had apparently been stolen. However, one of the investigating officers, knowing something of stamp collecting, discovered that there was a 2 cent Hawaii missing from the murdered man's collection; later, having become suspicious of one of the victim's friends, the detective effected an introduction to him as a fellow collector and the man subsequently showed him the stolen item. After arrest and failing to convince the police as to his legitimate ownership, he confessed to the murder.

Rare, but for the reason that only a few were produced for use, are the British Guiana 1850/51 issues, commonly referred to as the 'Cottonreels'. Produced locally in the offices of the *Royal Gazette*, the stamps were printed in black on coloured papers and were of such poor design and manufacture that, to guard against forgery, the postal clerks were instructed to initial each one when sold. A number of examples of 'Cottonreels' are in the collection, the rarest being the two cents rose, of which only a few items are known to have survived. However, whilst there are fourteen specimens recorded of the 4 cents on lemon-yellow, the example here is the only one recorded cut square on cover (**12**).

Rare errors

Of similar rarity is the error that occurred in the printing of the 1854 4d stamp of Western Australia (**15**). For some time after its discovery in 1863 it was referred to as the 'inverted swan'; however, it was subsequently established that it was the frame and not the centre that had been erroneously inverted. Only fourteen specimens of this error have come to light.

A similar type of error occurred with the India 4 annas issue of 1854 (**14**). This stamp was printed in two colours, the red frame being printed first; the error occurred when a few sheets were put through the printing press the wrong way round, resulting in the blue heads being inverted. It was twenty years before this 'inverted head' error was discovered and very few examples now exist. In the Tapling Collection can be seen two examples used on cover, these being the only ones known to exist in this form.

The error that occurred in a local printing in 1861 of the famous triangular stamps of the Cape of Good Hope was of a similar nature. The stamps were normally printed for the Colony by Perkins, Bacon & Company, London, but in 1861 a shortage of stamps occurred when a shipment was mislaid and, to cover the local need, Saul Solomon & Company of Cape Town were given an order to produce stamps which were of the same design as the normal London printings; in making up the plates from individual stereos, a 1d and a 4d stereo found their ways into the wrong plates, resulting in an error of colour in both of the values, the 1d appearing erroneously in blue and the 4d in red (**16**). From printing records it is known that 1194 examples of the 1d error were printed and 1568 of the 4d, but very few of these have survived.

Errors from mistakes in the assembly of plates are not uncommon. As has been seen, a number of them represent the major rarities of philately. But this is not so in the case of the *tête-bêche* items from the issues of France between 1849 and 1871 (**18**). These items are certainly rare, but they are not errors, for the plates were

16 *top and left*. Cape of Good Hope 1861 1d and 4d – errors of colour.

17 *above*. Spain 1851 2 reales – error of colour.

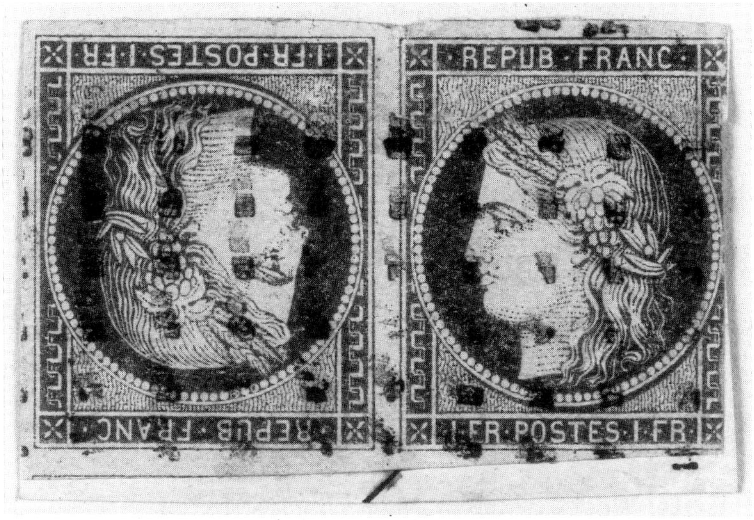

18 France 1849 1 Franc – *tête-bêche.*

assembled by Anatole Hulot, a strange man who worked in secrecy, and there is little doubt that he deliberately created the *tête-bêche* varieties in some of the plates by inverting some of the cliches.

This would almost certainly not have been the case with the 1851 2 reales issue of Spain, in which an error occurred in a similar manner to those of the Cape of Good Hope which have been previously described. The 2 reales cliche was put into the printing plate for the 6 reales and was consequently produced in blue instead of red (17); however, the error did not come to light for nearly 50 years, and it is of extreme rarity.

Exactly the same thing happened in the production of the 1872 issue of Sweden, only in this case the cliche was deliberately inserted. In this instance, just before the printing of the 20 öre was to commence, one of the cliches was found to be damaged; there being no substitute available, a cliche for the 30 öre was altered to '20' and used in the 20 öre printing. Unfortunately, the person who altered the cliche did not change the value in letters – which was 'tretio' – and some 1,600 sheets were released before the error was realised; before the Post Office could recover the stock, approximately 1,000 sheets had been sold. A very fine example of the 'tretio' used on piece can be seen in the collection (**19**).

There are occasions when stamps are prepared for use but, for one reason or another, are not issued; sometimes these unissued items can find their way into the hands of collectors and can be rare and very significant items; two such items which are of particular interest are to be found in the collection.

In 1863, a supply of 1/- stamps was sent to the colony of Barbados. These should have been printed in black, but they were

19 Sweden 1872–77 20 öre – tretio error.

20 New Brunswick
1860 5 cents –
Connell unissued.

found to have been erroneously printed in blue and were therefore not distributed for sale (**21**). The stock that was supplied was of 50,000 items, and it is not known what happened to these, other than the fact that approximately 10 found their way into the hands of collectors. Of similar status is a 5 cents stamp prepared in 1860 for New Brunswick, which was to be one of five denominations in a new issue for the change from sterling to decimal currency. The Postmaster-General of New Brunswick was Charles Connell and he selected the designs for the five values and gave instructions to the printers accordingly. The portraits of Queen Victoria and the Prince of Wales were to appear on the 10 and 17 cents respectively, whilst Connell decided that his own portrait would appear on the most commonly used value, the 5 cents (**20**). On delivery from the printers, the stamps were shown to the Governor of the province who ordered a delay of the issue. Connell subsequently resigned and bought the entire stock of the 5 cents stamps bearing his portrait, these having by now been replaced with new stamps bearing the Queen's portrait; after presenting a few of the unissued stamps to collector friends as souvenirs, Connell destroyed the balance, leaving a major rarity by which he is now remembered.

An exceptional rarity of Great Britain

The exceedingly rare 1858–79 Great Britain 1d issue printed from plate 77 is an example of rarity arising from production problems (**22**). This particular issue of 1d reds was perforated and the plate numbers can be seen in the frame ornamentation on each side. There were clearly problems in the platemaking for this issue as the first plate, number 69, could not be used, nor could number 70; stamps were printed from plate number 71, but again problems arose with plate numbers 75 and 77, only a few sheets being printed

21 Barbados 1863 1 shilling – error of colour.

22 Great Britain 1858–79 1d plate 77.

off each. Whilst no examples have ever been found from the printing from plate number 75, seven or eight examples have survived from the plate 77 printing of which the Tapling specimen is one of two examples in unused condition.

Great Britain

1890 General Post Office Christmas and New Year card, celebrating the Golden Jubilee of the Uniform Penny Postage.

23 Great Britain 1929 £1 Postal Union Congress – registration sheet.

It would be perfectly reasonable for the visitor to the British Library to assume that the Philatelic Collections would have strong sections of material relating to Great Britain. And this is certainly the case, with significant holdings of local and private posts and specialised collections as well as other postal material. The Tapling Collection, as described in the previous chapter, covers the whole world, and has a large section of superb Great Britain material. But the major holding of Great Britain material is that of the archives of the Stamping Department of the Board of Inland Revenue, which was placed on permanent loan with the British Museum in 1966, and covers a period from 1710 to the 1970s.

The Stamping Office

Established in 1694, the Stamp Office fulfilled the function of evidencing the payment of a huge range and variety of duties by the embossing and/or printing of duty stamps, licences, certificates, etc. This office is still operating today, but in a very limited way, as many of the areas of its work have been transferred to other Government departments, or else the duty is now accounted for other than by an embossed or adhesive stamp. Probably more than half of the archive relates to revenue material, but from 1840 until 1936 the Stamping Department of the Board of Inland Revenue was responsible for the production of postage stamps and stamped postal stationery for Great Britain and the overprinting of Great

24 Great Britain 1910 2d – unissued tyrian plum design.

STAMP OFFICE TICKET
For a day or days under 28.
G R
4
(No)
2 HORSES *for* ______ DAY
[*Let by or at*] ______
[*Of or In*] ______
The ______ *day of* ______ *18* ______
****
[*If so hired*] *To go to* ______
and back, being ______ *Miles.*
If hired for 2 or more Days, Name and Residence of Hirer to be written on the back.
STAMP OFFICE TICKET

25 Great Britain Horse Licence.

26 *right.* Great Britain 1912 (1 Jan) 1d – offset printing.

Britain stamps for use in certain overseas territories.

The sheer volume of material makes it difficult to give the reader a full description of its scope, for within the archive are all forms of preparatory material such as artists' drawings, trials, essays, die proofs, hundreds of sheets of black plate proofs, registration sheets, etc. It represents a fundamental source for the researcher. But as well as its use as a research source, there are a great many fascinating and exquisitely engraved items in the collection which provide interest. These were produced for duties, such as Hair Powder tax, or as licences, for example for Armorial Bearings or for the hire of horses (**25**), and other such activities of a bygone age.

From the point of view of the philatelist, notable items are the beautiful colour trials of 1913, which include unissued colours and the use of the die from which was prepared the extremely rare Edward VII 2d tyrian plum (**24**), never issued due to the King's death in 1910. Quite spectacular are some of the complete sheets of George V low values in unissued colours or designs, particularly one of the 1d value completely – and seemingly deliberately – offset (**26**). The registration sheets also give one the opportunity to see items in a form not otherwise seen. This is particularly so in respect

CANCELLED

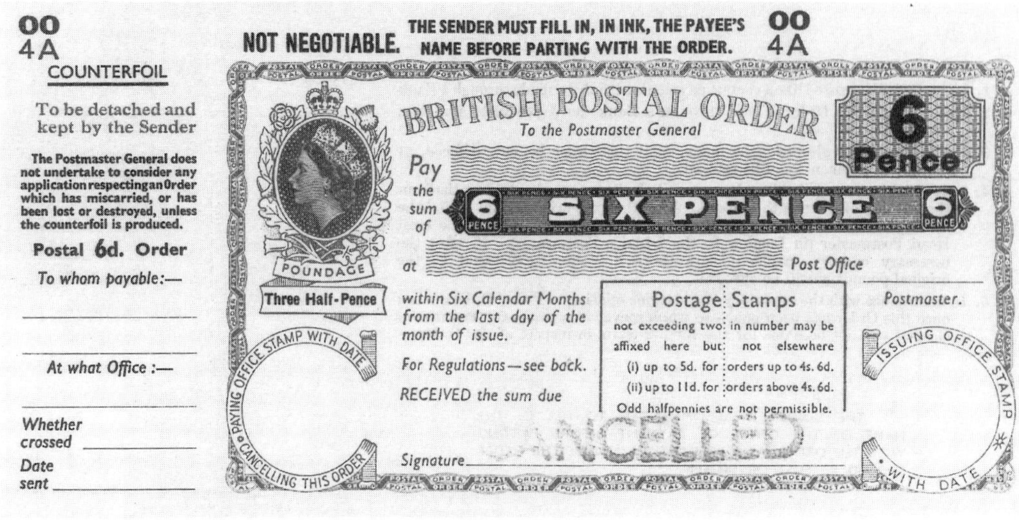
OO
4A
COUNTERFOIL
To be detached and kept by the Sender
The Postmaster General does not undertake to consider any application respecting an Order which has miscarried, or has been lost or destroyed, unless the counterfoil is produced.
Postal 6d. Order
To whom payable:—
At what Office :—
Whether crossed
Date sent
NOT NEGOTIABLE. THE SENDER MUST FILL IN, IN INK, THE PAYEE'S NAME BEFORE PARTING WITH THE ORDER.
OO
4A
BRITISH POSTAL ORDER
To the Postmaster General
6 Pence
Pay the sum of
6 PENCE SIX PENCE 6 PENCE
POUNDAGE
Three Half-Pence
at
Post Office
Postmaster.
within Six Calendar Months from the last day of the month of issue.
For Regulations—see back.
RECEIVED the sum due
Signature
Postage Stamps
not exceeding two in number may be affixed here but not elsewhere
(i) up to 5d. for orders up to 4s. 6d.
(ii) up to 11d. for orders above 4s. 6d.
Odd halfpennies are not permissible.
CANCELLED
PAYING OFFICE STAMP WITH DATE CANCELLING THIS ORDER
ISSUING OFFICE STAMP WITH DATE

27 Great Britain Queen Elizabeth II 6d postal order proof.

to the complete imperforate sheet of the 1929 Postal Union Congress £1 (23) and other high value postage stamps, as well as items now long gone from public memory, such as National Savings and National Insurance stamps; it is in these latter two areas that the collection of material of Her Majesty's Stationery Office has its main strength, containing not only the issued stamps, but preparatory material as well. As well as supplementing the Inland Revenue material, the HMSO Collection contains additional items from the past, now long forgotten – items such as the stamps that were prepared for the imposition (never carried out) of a luxury tax, just after the 1914–18 war; or, more recently, the petrol coupons that were issued during the oil crisis in 1956 as the result of the Suez conflict, and those that were prepared and issued (but, again, not used) during the 1960s oil crisis.

The HMSO Collection also contains substantial amounts of material relating to postal orders, both the preparatory material and the issued postal orders, and including essays and proofs (27). This collecting area is now gaining strength as the result of its close association with the portraits of successive monarchs as used on revenue and postage stamps.

Railway services

When Sydney R. Turner bequeathed some of his collections to the British Museum in 1973, he probably did not appreciate how well the smallest one would be received; it is a specialised collection of the duty dies for the 6d and 2/6d revenues from 1694, serving to fill the gap of sixteen years at the beginning of the Inland Revenue archive. This was not the only collection of Turner to bridge a gap, for his collection of British railway letter and parcel stamps represents a substantial addition to the large collection of similar material formed by H. L'Estrange Ewen which had already been donated to the British Museum in 1949.

The Ewen Collection represents by far the largest public holding of this material. It is highly specialised in the way in which it was formed, consisting mainly of reconstructions of sheets of stamps for virtually every railway company and joint line committee from 1891 to 1912. Whilst it does contain covers, the main strength of railway covers is to be found in the Turner Collection, which also extends the period to the mid 1940s.

The issue of railway letter stamps commenced on 1 February 1891 (prior to that time, the railway companies had only been able to carry parcels). The companies earned good revenue by operating a letter carrying service which was very efficient and rapid. The system operated in this way; a letter would be taken by the sender to a station and the appropriate fee paid. The sender was often able to stipulate the time of the train on which it was to be carried. This latter point was important because, on arrival, the letter could be collected by the addressee (**29**) or, as the sender had affixed the correct normal postage stamps for onward transmission, it would be posted in the normal manner in the post box nearest to the station of arrival. The service was fast and well used by those who needed rapid carriage of letters over long distances; some companies offered special services to people such as newspaper employees for the express sending of reports or photographs to their editors.

During the life of the private companies, virtually all of them operated such a service and, with the amalgamation of companies and lines, well over a hundred different issuing authorities are recorded.

28 Lundy Island 1939 10th anniversary overprints.

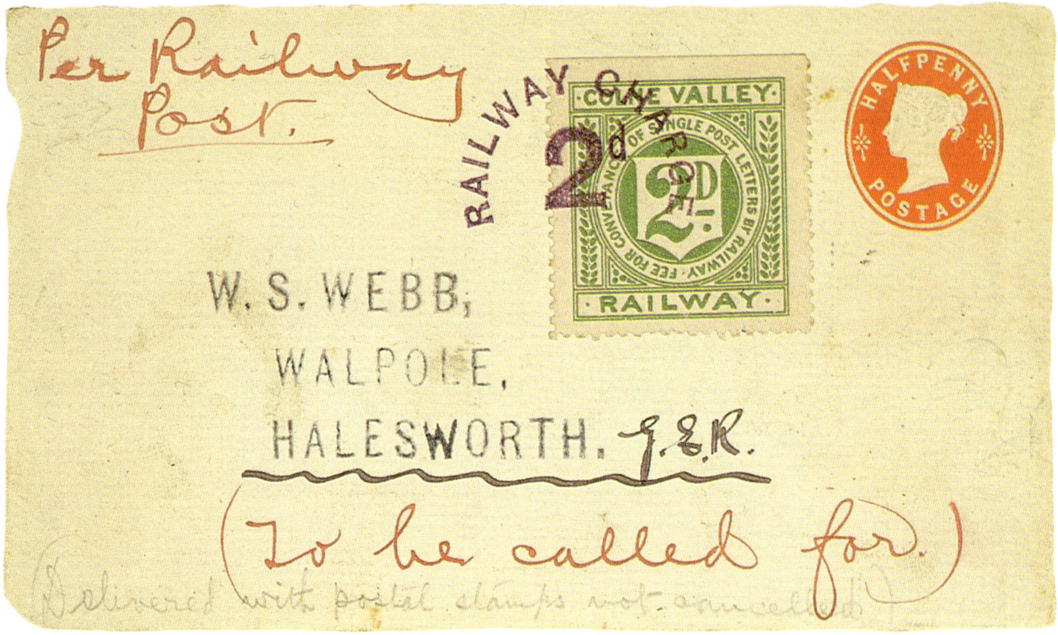

29 A railway letter.

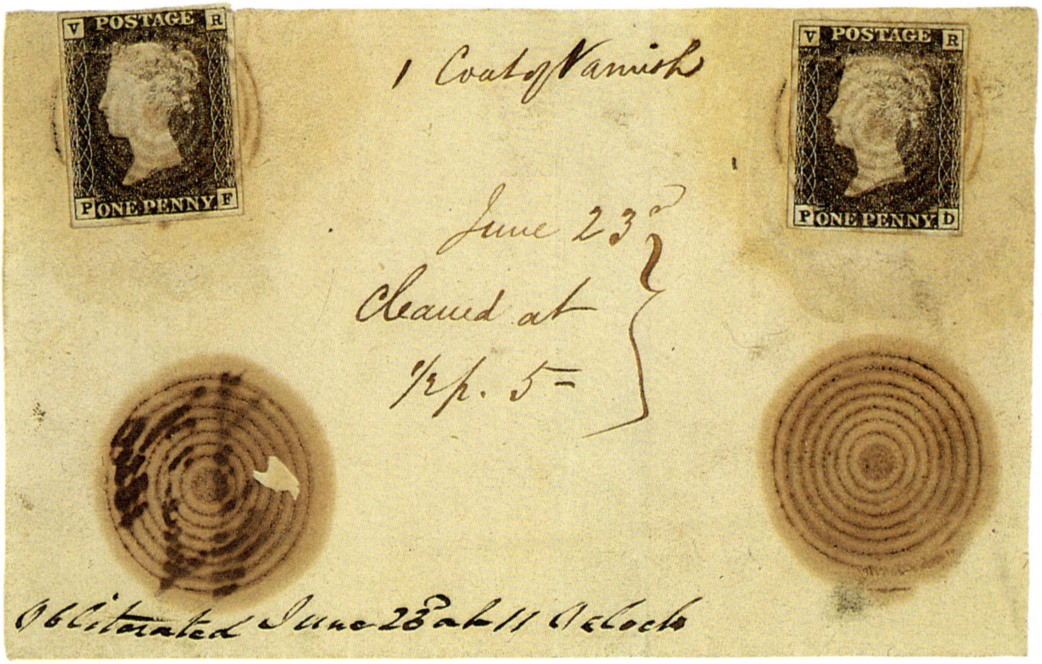

30 Great Britain. Two 1840 'VR' 1d blacks with experimental cancellations.

Another private service which is justifiably well represented at the British Library is that of Lundy Island, a small island situated in the Bristol Channel near to the North Devon coast. Lundy Island has operated a private service since 1928, after the Post Office withdrew in 1927. It is not a total service and, in some respects, has some similarity to that operated by the railway companies. Letters are paid by Lundy stamps (28) for carriage to or from the Island to Barnstaple, Ilfracombe or Instow, where they are collected or put into the mails; as with railway letters, they must carry a GB postage stamp to pay for onward transmission to the North Devon ports or to the addressees.

The collection is probably the only one of its type in public hands and, almost certainly, the finest extant of this often difficult material; it was given to the British Library in 1977 by Barry Chinchen who had assembled it over a number of years both as a collector and to serve as a record of his work as the philatelic agent for the lessees of the Island, the Landmark Trust. The collection contains a considerable wealth of material including stamps, proofs, artwork, and covers, and continues to grow with the addition by Mr Chinchen of the new issues.

31 College stamp – Keble College, Oxford.

Rare and unusual

There is a large section of GB material in the Tapling Collection and this, as one would expect, contains ranges of the printings from the plates for the 1840 and 1841 1d and 2d stamps as well as examples from later plates of other issues. One could go into great detail about the many rare and exciting items to be found there, for example the two 'VR' 1d blacks on a piece of paper with trial cancellations and annotated by Rowland Hill (**30**); the 'VR' stamps were prepared for official use but were never issued, and are so described because they have the same design as the 1840 1d black, with the exception that the letters 'V' and 'R' are inserted in the upper corners in place of the normal crosses.

Mention has already been made (see page **23**) of the great rarity of the 1d plate 77, but not of the so-called 'abnormals'. These were stamps which came from plates that were not issued and arose from registration sheets from the plates finding their way into stock, and being perforated and issued in the normal way.

However, many of the more obscure items in the Collection are equally worthy of examination, particularly those prepared for official and private telegraph services, the circular delivery companies and the colleges of Oxford and Cambridge. The latter were first issued in 1871 and continued in use until 1887, at which time their use was challenged by the Postmaster General as being a breach of the Post Office monopoly. The stamps carried no denomination in their design, which consisted of the college name and crest and were intended for use on mail carried by college messengers; most of these stamps are scarce and some are rare, particularly when found used on cover (**31**).

The Tapling Collection contains virtually a complete range of postage, revenue, semi-official and private stamps of GB for virtually the first fifty years of the adhesive stamp, and it is an area which will richly reward careful examination.

Specialised collections

1940–41 Guernsey. 1d artwork, signed by the designer E.W. Vaudin. Used during the German occupation of the Channel Islands.

AMBASADA ST. Z. J. AMERYKI
WARSZAWA WRZESIEŃ 1939
POCZTA POLSKA Gr 5

MINISTERSTWO SKARBU
WARSZAWA WRZESIEŃ 1939
POCZTA POLSKA Gr 10

ZBURZENIE POMNIKA
MICKIEWICZA KRAKÓW 1940
POCZTA POLSKA Gr 25

PLAC ZAMKOWY WARSZAWA WRZESIEŃ 1939
POCZTA POLSKA Gr 55

WOJSKO POLSKIE W W. BRYTANII
POCZTA POLSKA Gr 75

POLSKA BROŃ PANCERNA W W. BRYTANII
POCZTA POLSKA Gr 80

POLSKA MARYNARKA
WOJENNA W W. BRYTANII
O.R.P. "ORZEŁ"
Zł 1
Gr 50 POCZTA POLSKA

LOTNICTWO POLSKIE W W. BRYTANII
POCZTA POLSKA Zł 1

Over the years, the nature and form of collecting has changed. Originally, the Victorians were able to collect the stamps of the whole world to a reasonable degree of completeness and, for this reason, the average collectors were not selective in their interest; however, it would be virtually impossible to collect in this way today, because of the vast sums of money that would be required to keep up with the new issues alone. This situation has been progressive in its effect, with the serious collectors initially restricting their interests to, perhaps, groups of countries, or specific periods of time or a particular field of interest. For some years now, it has been more a case of the serious collector restricting interest to a particular period within a country. But at all periods there have always been exceptions to the general rule.

In 1919, the Trustees of the British Museum were presented with what was then described as the most important collection of stamps since that of Tapling in 1891; this was a specialised collection of the stamps of Siam which had been formed by R. W. Harold Row, BSC, FLS, FZS, FRPSL, who had died earlier that year, and covers a period from 1883 to 1918.

Harold Row and Siam

Row was appreciated as being the authority on the stamps of Siam by his peers. His studies of the surcharges was to such a depth that it is unlikely that the importance of his collection and his knowledge of these difficult issues will be surpassed.

The surcharges gave rise to rare types and errors, and also produced curiosities, not the least of which was the '1 tical' surcharge

33 Siam 1885 1 tical surcharge on 1 solot.

32 Poland 1944 London issues.

on the 1 solot denomination of the first issue (33). Normally, when a need to surcharge has arisen, it has been either for the purpose of overcoming a shortage of a high usage denomination or to change the denomination of stamps in the event of a change of currency. The selection of the stamps for surcharging is usually made from excess stocks of low usage stamps, often of a substantially higher face value. In the case of the '1 tical' surcharge, it had the effect of increasing the stamps' original value by 128 times; the opportunity to defraud the Post Office by forging the surcharge was something that was certainly not missed by some local people at the time! Such is the nature of these overprints that it is difficult to determine which of these surcharges are genuine or otherwise; but for the excellent work of Row in unravelling this problem, the collectors of today would be confronted with a much more difficult task in isolating the forgeries that were identified by him.

In addition to the extensive study on the surcharges, Row's collection also includes essays, proofs, substantial amounts of postal stationery and examples of Siamese stamps used in Kedah and Kelantan, both now part of Malaysia.

The collection taken as a whole represents a fine example of an early highly specialised study of a single country.

34 Wei Hai Wei
1899 2 cents.

China and its local posts

Although not as intensive a study as Row's, the collection of China which was formed by Engineer Captain J. A. Murray, RN, and presented by his grandson, Mr Maurice Murray, in 1980, was formed at approximately the same time and again, like Row's, is the only collection of its type in public hands. The Murray Collection of China today is only one of two collections of the material that were formed at the time and that are still intact. It was assembled by Murray in the closing years of the last century whilst he was serving on board HMS *Iphiginia* on China station; his preoccupation with the local stamps and postal services attracted the attention of one of the other officers who allegedly acquired a small sack of stamps and covers whilst on shore and passed them on to Murray to occupy his spare time, there being little else to do. Murray kept up to date with all the new issues that appeared in the local offices, and sought out obsolete material as well. He was well placed to obtain fine examples of the local post service of Wei Hai Wei (**34**), which at the time was a British protectorate and initially operated the local service using stamps produced by a local firm, Cornabe & Co. The collection also includes excellent examples of the provisional issues of Foochow and Chungking as well as an invaluable assemblage of the 1897 surcharges on the Customs stamps.

Upon his death, the collection passed to his son, Dr S. E. Murray, who continued to add to it. At this time, the collection started to lose the character of the material that had formed it, for Dr Murray did not have the advantages of availability that his father had had; however, significant additions were made when possible, and the collection now extends to the mid 1950s.

Poland in the Second World War

Another form of specialisation is demonstrated by the collection of Polish history from 1938 to 1949, which was presented to the British Museum in 1966 by the late M. A. Bojanowicz. Whilst entitled 'Polish Postal History', it extends way beyond the postal history of Poland as a country by giving a graphic account of the Polish people, in all their activities, during that most difficult time in their history.

The Poles, and in a similar way, the Czechs, have always placed great importance on the maintenance of postal communications, especially in times of national difficulty or crisis, and have always appreciated the importance of maintaining an unimpaired and independent service, the most recent demonstration of this being the underground postal services of Solidarity in Poland. The Bojanowicz Collection shows in depth the efforts of the Poles to maintain their independence, even after the occupation of their country by Nazi German forces in 1939, and includes examples of

35 Burglengenfeld. Commemoration of the liberation of Dachau concentration camp.

36 Germany 1946 obliterated Hitler stamp.

37 *right*. Germany 1946 Finsterwalde local issue.

artwork, essays, proofs, issued and used material which was produced in the ghettos, and the internment and concentration camps (35).

The Polish armed forces who left their homeland to continue the fight as part of the Allied Forces were deployed in many of the theatres of war and operated from a number of countries; in virtually all of these they operated their own field postal services, identifiable by the cancellers they produced and used, and which were also used in conjunction with stamps and patriotic labels. There is an abundance of these in the collection and they trace, in a fascinating way, the movement of the Polish Free Forces during the war, both in their active service, and in the posts they operated in the German prisoner of war camps.

Between 1941 and 1944, four issues of Polish stamps were produced for the exiled government in London (32); these stamps were used on Polish ships and permission was given for their use in Polish military camps in Great Britain; the preparatory material for these stamps can be seen in this collection, amongst which are some superb life-size items of artwork.

The Allied occupation of Germany

In 1945, the Allies occupied Germany, and this immediately created problems for the civil population with respect to the postal service; a system, albeit disrupted, was still available to them, but the only stamps on sale at the post offices were the current issues of the Hitler regime, principally those which bore Hitler's portrait. The use of these stamps in unaltered form on the mail in occupied Germany was totally unacceptable to the Allied Military Commanders, so local postmasters, not having yet received the Allied issues

38 Germany 1948 currency reform overprint.

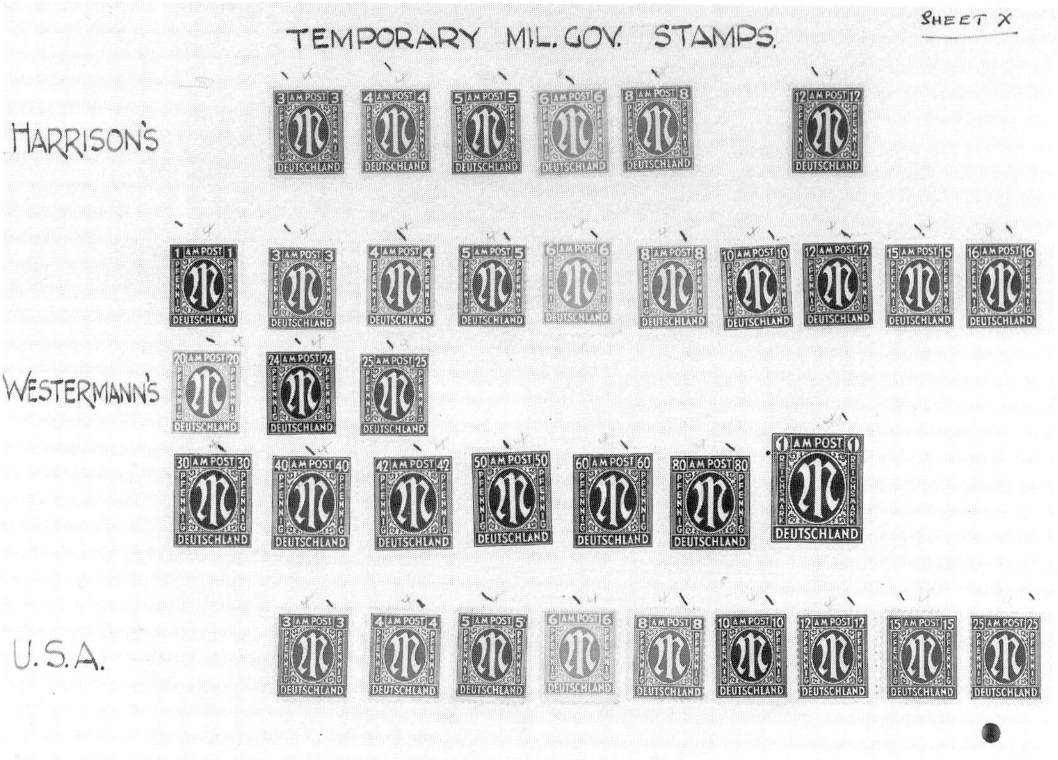

39 Germany 1946 Allied Military Government issues.

and having no other stamps available to them, nor having the means to produce new designs quickly, produced a variety of ways of obliterating the Hitler portrait or Nazi swastika, which then made them acceptable for use (**36**).

In 1956, Dr Walther Model von Thunen presented the British Museum with a collection of these provisional issues which had been used during 1945 and 1946; the collection is virtually complete and shows the very many defacers (all identifiable to a particular town) which were used by local postmasters. As time passed, some towns were able to replace the unsatisfactory Hitler stamps with new locally designed and issued stamps (**37**), which vary considerably in their quality of design and production; these continued in official use until they were replaced by the unified issues which were released in February 1946 by the Allied Military Government, once it had re-established the nationally regulated system.

In the same year that Model presented his collection to the British Museum, the British Foreign Office made a gift of a collection of material that had been brought back from Germany with the records of the British Military Government. The importance of this material is that it bridges the gap between the 1945/46 local issues of

Model and the first issues of the civilian government which were released in September 1949. The postal history of this period is complicated by the variations of issues which occurred in the Russian and French zones of Germany; however, the issues covered in the collection are those which were used in the British and American zones and generally in all four. The chronology of the stamp-issuing in Germany during this period starts in Aachen in March 1945, when the British and American forces issued stamps in their zones which were inscribed 'AM post', that is the Allied Military Government post. During this time, local stamps were used in the Russian and French zones. All these stamps remained in use until they were replaced by a unified issue which was released throughout all of the zones in February 1946. This latter issue was a simple design carrying a numeral representing the denomination in the centre.

In March 1947 a new definitive series of five different designs was released and continued in use until withdrawn on 24 June 1948. It was at this point that the Russian zone issues became separate from those of the British, American and French zones as the result of a reform of the currency in the latter three zones. The change was sudden and unexpected and to effect the currency change on the stamps, in what has now become West Germany, some of the unified issue stamps were overprinted with a posthorn pattern (38). These continued in use until new definitives inscribed 'Deutsche Post' and in the changed currency, were released in September 1948. These were used until replaced by the first issue of the civil government, which was established in September 1949.

As well as the definitives that were released in this period, four commemorative issues appeared, these being the 50th anniversary of the death of Heinrich Stephan, founder of the Universal Postal Union in 1874, which was released on 15 May 1947; four stamps for the Leipzig Autumn and Spring Fairs on the 2 September 1947 and 2 March 1948 respectively, and the Hannover Export Exhibition on 22 May 1948.

The collection contains many proofs and registration sheets of these issues, which are not known to exist elsewhere and provide a fascinating insight into this short but important and interesting period in the history of Germany's postal service.

AIR MAIL
U S POSTAGE
16
This stamp is

Airmails

1934–36 United States. Air Special Delivery stamp. Designed and annotated by Franklin D. Roosevelt, the US President at the time.

Man flies

Since man first left the ground to fly in balloons, the possibilities for speeding up the mails by air has been appreciated, as it had been with the railways and other forms of transport. The age of the aeroplane made the possibility a reality, although it was the earlier balloon flights that proved the system.

The collecting of items of mail carried by air is an area which has slowly gained strength over the years, after very slow beginnings; although a few collectors would have collected items at the time of the early pioneer flights, the existence of much of that material today is due to the fact that it was kept as a curiosity or souvenir. These early souvenirs stem mainly from the early air meetings (**40**) or pioneer flights. Pilots would carry picture postcards, specially prepared for the event and usually bearing a photograph of the pilot and/or his aircraft, and these they would quite often sign and sell to defray the costs of a flight.

Today, some of these souvenirs represent the only remaining record of some of the smaller and more obscure aviation meetings, and the less significant pioneer flights. Whilst they are historically interesting, they are not significant to the purist who is only interested in the history of the development of the post; however, while its reputation does not benefit from the fact that so much has been created with collectors in mind, the vast majority of the material is significant. Its high significance rests in the fact that it demonstrates how the present day carriage of mail by air has developed since those early beginnings. The British Library is indeed fortunate in possessing what are probably the finest collections of air post material in public hands.

Mrs Augustine Fitzgerald

In 1942, Mrs Augustine Fitzgerald offered her collection of world airmails to the British Museum Trustees. The collection is outstanding and contains a host of rarities, but at that time was only really known to a few collectors who were interested in aerophilately. Mrs Fitzgerald, understanding the value and importance of the collection, wished it to be placed in the safekeeping of an institution that would not disperse it.

At the time it was offered, the Museum collections were securely stored for the wartime conditions that prevailed, and it was not until 1947 that the eighteen-volume collection was delivered. It is indeed a truly remarkable assemblage of material, and must stand very high in the league of the great aerophilatelic collections. To attempt to describe the large number of rare items within it would require a book in itself and it is difficult to have to omit mention of so many; however, among the groups of material in the collection, by far the largest is that of the balloon posts from the sieges of Metz and Paris in the Franco–Prussian war of 1870–71.

40 Great Britain 1910 souvenir postcard of Blackpool air meeting.

The sieges of Metz and Paris

The siege of Metz started at the beginning of September 1870, just five weeks after the outbreak of war, and continued until the surrender of the French troops there on 28 October. In an effort to pass news out of the city, unmanned balloons carrying mail were released; the mail took the form of letter sheets in envelopes made from very thin paper to keep the weight to a minimum (**41**). The first balloons used could each carry a load of about 200 letters; later in the siege, much larger ballons were used which could carry a payload of more than a hundred times the size of the early ones. Many of the balloons were shot down by the Prussians, and in consequence items flown out from the siege are today rare survivors.

After the French surrender at Sedan, and the Prussian siege of Metz in September 1870, the Third Republic was declared and a new government was established in Paris, which by then found itself cut off from the rest of France. As at Metz, there was the same problem of maintaining lines of communication. At first, hollow metal balls containing letters were put into the River Seine to float downstream; as with the balloons, they were shot at by the Prussians and sank, becoming embedded in the mud of the river bed or

41 France 1870 – 'Papillon de Metz'.

banks. (It is not known how many of these were launched but even today they are still being recovered from the river.)

The next method was to use balloons. Some already existed in the city; and further balloons were constructed during the siege. All of the 65 balloons that left Paris during the siege were manned. Substantial quantities of mail and newspapers were carried out, the latter being printed on special flimsy paper for the purpose. The siege balloon posts also produced the first recorded air post cancellations, being those which were applied to letters by the balloon manufacturers, Nadar-Dartois-Duruof, later Dartois & Yon. The cancellation bearing the names is exceedingly rare, only three such items having come to light. An example of this cancellation appears in the collection (**42**), together with a large range of mail carried by different balloons.

In addition to the mail carried out by the balloons, they also transported carrier pigeons, and it was the use of these that gave rise to the earliest form of microfilm. Initially, the pigeons carried despatches, converted into microphotographic form, but later, as the system developed, private mail was also carried by this method (**43**).

42 France 1870–71 Siege of Paris – Nadar-Dartois-Duruof cachet.

The first trans-Atlantic flight

Another fascinating and rare group of material in this collection is that which relates to the first air mail carried across the Atlantic from Newfoundland in 1919. This was the result of the offer of a prize of £10,000 by Lord Northcliffe, proprietor of the *Daily Mail*, for the first non-stop flight. Four teams were to make the attempt, each one carrying some mail, but only three were actually in time for the competition. The winning team was that of Captain John Alcock and Lieutenant Arthur Whitton-Brown, who completed their journey by crash-landing their modified Vickers Vimy bomber near Clifden, in western Ireland, just 16 hours 12 minutes after leaving St Johns, Newfoundland on 14 June 1919.

Examples of the mail carried by Alcock and Brown and the other competitors, together with other memorabilia, are to be found in this collection, and they are all of the highest rarity (**44**).

The collection abounds with rare items from pioneer flights, some of which were dogged with problems and others of which ended in tragedy. One of the latter was the pioneer flight that left Harbour Grace, Newfoundland on 5 September 1927, and was

43 France 1870–71 Siege of Paris – souvenir reproduction of despatch carried by pigeon.

never seen again. The flight was sponsored by the President of Carling Breweries Ltd., and was to travel from London, Ontario to London, England; the pilot, Captain Tulley, was carrying 97 items of mail, each bearing one of the special stamps that had been prepared for the flight. Of the three remaining examples of the stamps, two are in this collection (**45**).

44 Pilot's licence of Captain John Alcock.

No. 269 Class A.

C.A. Form 8.

AIR MINISTRY.

Air Navigation Acts, 1911 to 1919

Name John Alcock, K.B.E., D.S.C.,
Address Weybridge Works, Byfleet Rd, Weybridge.
Nationality British.
Is hereby licensed as Pilot [of aircraft not carrying passengers or goods for hire or reward]
of the ...... class of aircraft
for a period of Six months from
the Nineteenth day of August 1919
to the Eighteenth day of February 1920.
inclusive, subject to the Orders made by the Secretary of State under the Air Navigation Acts, 1911 to 1919.

Air Ministry, London, W.C. 2.

Secretary of the Air Council.

PHOTOGRAPH OF HOLDER.

Signature of holder J. Alcock.

N.B.—This licence is not transferable nor can it be used for any class or classes of aircraft other than the class or classes specified herein.

Italian Levant air post

The rarest item in the collection was prepared for use on a service that was never actually operated. In December 1921, the Italian Post Office at Constantinople made arrangements with a French company for the latter to extend the air post service which it operated to Paris from Constantinople, to provide a service to Italy as well. On this basis, the local Italian Postmaster set arrangements in hand to have a quantity of the Italian 1903 25 cent Express stamp overprinted with a biplane, and surcharged 15 piastre (**46**). The overprinting was carried out by the Italian printers D'Andria, who had handled the overprinting of other Italian stamps. But before the service had commenced, the French Ambassador and the Post Office stepped in to forbid the new air post service, insisting that everything had to be directed through the local French Administration.

There was nothing more that the Italian Post Office could do, except to suspend the overprinting and abandon the project, those stamps that had already been overprinted being destroyed. In fact, some of the stamps did survive, and six or seven are known to exist. The one that appears in this collection differs from the others and is authenticated as the accepted essay for the overprint.

In spite of the strength of the collection in virtually every country, its noticeable weakness is in the British airmails; this is not because Mrs Fitzgerald did not acquire the material, but rather because in leaving France in 1940, that particular volume was lost. It was 30 years before the gap was filled, but in spectacular fashion,

45 Newfoundland 1927. London – London semi-official stamp.

46 Italian Levant 1921. Essay for an airmail stamp.

47 Great Britain 1911 Coronation flights, London – Windsor.

when in 1977 Mr H. Eric Scott donated his superb collection of the British inland airmails to the British Library.

British inland air posts

The richness of Mr Scott's collection derives from the fact that he commenced his collecting in 1930, at a time when very few people were actively collecting air post material. This gave him the opportunity to acquire rare items for little cost, as their importance or rarity at that time was not appreciated by other collectors or the vast majority of the philatelic trade. Mr Scott's collection is formidable in both size and content and is quite unsurpassed.

It is hard to select any particular area as representing the major strength, for it is strong in virtually all areas. There are, for example, a number of volumes of pioneer flights, others for the 1911 London–Windsor flights, and specific major air meetings or competitions.

The collection spans a period from the late eighteenth century to the 1970s; virtually all of the pioneer flight and souvenirs from the early air meetings are present, as well as flown souvenirs from other events, the rarest being a flown unofficial card from the 1902 Beckenham Coronation Celebration balloon flight, this item being only one of six believed to have survived (**47**).

48 Beckenham 1902 Coronation celebrations balloon flight.

In 1911, an airmail service was set up from London to Windsor as part of the celebrations for the Coronation of King George V; special postal cards and envelopes were printed in a range of different colours and sold for the service (**48**). The collection has a large specialised study of these items and includes a number of related ephemeral items. The same applies to the section of the collection devoted to the 1912 *Daily Mail* 'Circuit of Britain', which attracted a number of famous early aviators, and this section abounds with the souvenirs of their flights (**49**).

A somewhat obscure study is that of airmail etiquettes, the familiar blue adhesive airmail labels for letters, and there is a very comprehensive section of these within the collection. The nature and content of this section is such that it is arguably the finest assembly of this material anywhere, and almost certainly the only one of its kind in public hands.

South African pioneer airmails

Specialisation appears in areas of the Scott Collection, but the Monks Collection of South African airmails is a case of pure specialisation. The collection encompasses the period from 1911 to about 1960 and was bequeathed to the British Library in 1981. David Monks joined the Royal Navy in the boys' service shortly after leaving school in 1946, and served throughout the world dur-

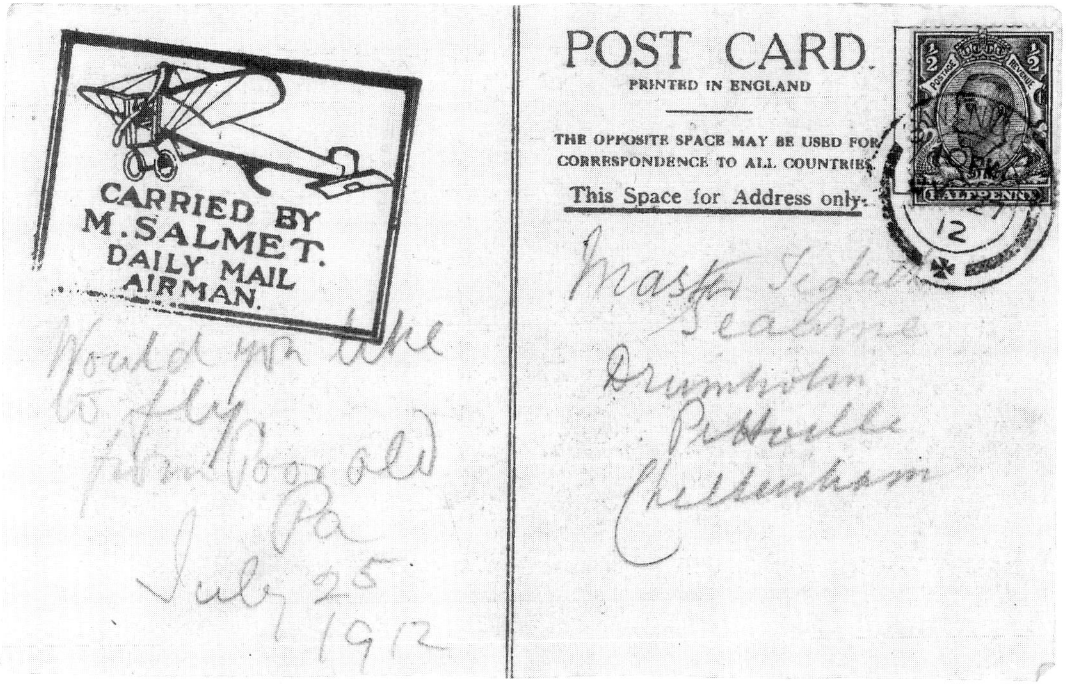

49 Postcard from the 'Daily Mail' 1912 'Circuit of Britain' flights.

ing his 33 years' service. He had many interests and pastimes, but his consuming interest was his collection of South African airmails, which was systematically collected to ensure completeness of the pioneer and inaugural flights, for example those of Imperial Airways and South African Airways. The collection is remarkable in this respect.

A classic example of a pioneer flight appears in the collection. Unlike some others, the surviving items of mail arose purely from a need and not the demand of collectors (**50**). The story of this attempted service gives a fine insight into the difficulties that confronted many of these early flights. On 15 February 1920 at 6.30 am a converted Handley Page 400 bomber left Wynburg Airport with a crew of three and seven passengers to travel from Cape Town to Johannesburg. It landed at a farm to check its course and later had to make a forced landing at Blaauwheuvel because of a damaged fuel tank; as the result of this fault, petrol had been lost and more had to be brought, but the nearest place where some was available was fifty miles away. The aircraft reached Laingsbury on 17 February and extra fuel was sent there from Beaufort West, which was to be the first official stop, and this was made at 11 am on 19 February. At 1.30 pm that same day, the aircraft left on the next stage of its journey, but eight minutes after take-off a rudder post broke and a crash landing was made in swampy ground. The aircraft was so

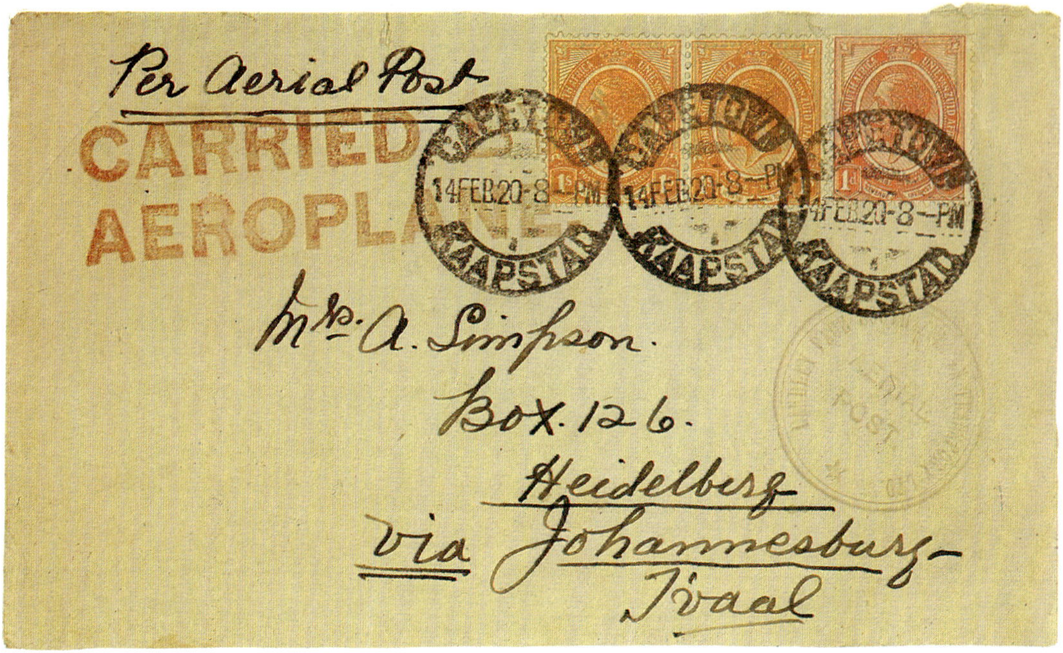

50 Envelope carried on the fated 1920 Cape Town to Johannesburg flight.

badly damaged that it could not continue the journey, and the mail that was being carried completed its journey by train.

The mail from this flight had a cachet applied in large letters, 'CARRIED BY AEROPLANE', and although 422 items were taken on at Cape Town and a further 17 at Beaufort West, only 20 are now known to exist.

Today we take airmail services for granted, never perhaps realising the hardships and dangers to life that occurred in those early days; but a browse through the stories of the pioneer flights – and the airmail items which serve to commemorate them – should make us all appreciate the sacrifices that were made to establish a future which we now enjoy.

Right. 1935 King George V Silver Jubilee issues. Approved and rejected colour proofs.

1
9
1910-1935
POSTAGE & REVENUE
2
10
3
11
4

In reviewing what one might term the 'general' philatelic collections in the British Library, one would always come back to the Tapling Collection as being the one of prime importance; however, there are other collections of a general nature, with different material of considerable significance.

The Supplementary Collection

After 1891 and the much publicised bequest of the Tapling Collection, a number of valuable donations were received by the British Museum, the first arriving in July 1900 when the Crown Agents presented three albums to the Trustees. These albums contained colonial material which included rare De La Rue proofs and essays (58). From October of that same year, the Crown Agents commenced sending to the British Museum examples of all new colonial stamps whose production th y had arranged, and that arrangement continues to the present day.

In 1914 a very large donation was received from the Postmaster-General which comprised specimens of stamps, envelopes and postcards for a number of countries, and which had originated from the Universal Postal Union at Berne. In addition to these, a number of smaller donations had also been received and it was decided that all of this material should be brought together in a single collection.

This collection, known as the Supplementary Collection, was mounted and captioned by Edward Bacon on similar leaves to those he had used for the Tapling Collection, and these were housed in the now redundant album binders of the Tapling Collection (for it was 1922 before Bacon's work on this collection was completed).

Whilst the collection is somewhat haphazard in its content, it does contain very many rare and important items, particularly those from former British colonies.

In 1916 the Government of India presented four copper plates and nine lithographic stones to the Royal Philatelic Society, London. Four sets of impressions were taken from the plates and stones by Messrs. Perkins, Bacon & Co. Ltd., prior to their defacing them in September of that year, and a set of the impressions were presented to the British Museum by the Royal Philatelic Society London. The set of impressions are mounted in this collection (51).

The St Helena section contains a number of interesting items. For example, of the 1863 issue, there are no less than 14 examples of the 6d blue, watermark large star, imperforate together with essays of the surcharge that was used on the 1d and 4d stamps. Most of these are exceedingly rare, as is the 1911 1d red pictorial stamp bearing the portrait of King Edward VII, which was prepared for

51 India 1854
½ anna – pull from
the original die.

use but not issued and, whilst examples are known overprinted 'Specimen', very few are known without the overprint, as is the case with the example in this collection (**52**).

The Universal Postal Union and the Crown Agents

On permanent loan from the Post Office is a collection of major importance to researchers and collectors alike; it is the collection of 'Specimens' or unused stamps received from the member nations of the Universal Postal Union, which are distributed from the headquarters of the organisation at Berne, Switzerland. Under the terms of their membership, postal administrations are obliged to send in sufficient examples of new issues, valid for international use, to the UPU for distribution to other member administrations.

Distributions are made on a regular basis and represent an annual growth of the British Library's collection of about 10,000 items per annum. The importance of the collection as a reference source stems from the manner in which it was formed and continues to grow, being composed entirely of material received from the issuing authorities; as such, it is unquestionably authentic.

Mention has already been made of the Crown Agents Collection; the material donated by the Crown Agents from 1900 to 1922 was mounted up into the Supplementary Collection, but since that time it has been kept as a collection in its own right, and grows in a similar manner to the UPU Collection, being all the material produced by the Crown Agents for their clients.

The other aspect of the Crown Agents material is that which is contained within the Philatelic and Security Printing archive. This

52 St Helena 1911 1d red pictorial – not issued.

53 Pitcairn Island 1964 6d – finished artwork.

54 Wembley Empire Exhibition 1924–25 – progressive die proofs showing change of year.

is a major source for researchers, and contains essays, artwork (53), proofs, colour trials and the records relating to the whole range of work associated with postage and revenue stamps, postal stationery, postal orders and currency notes. The archive commences at about 1900 and extends to the present time. It contains a vast quantity of exceptionally rare items, including material that was produced for use, but which was never actually issued.

John A. C. Harrison – an exceptional engraver

The techniques used in the production of stamps are extensively demonstrated in the Crown Agents archive. So, in a limited, but no less interesting, way is the engraver's preparatory material for the production of stamps which appears in the Harrison Collection of die proofs. John A. C. Harrison, was born in 1872 and was the son of the engraver Samuel Harrison, from whom he learned his craft. The collection of Harrison's engraved die proofs of postage stamps was donated to the British Museum by his son, Herbert W. P. Harrison, in 1963. It represents a range of the large variety of work which he produced, and displays his remarkable skills in the engraving of many different types of subjects – including portraits, figure work, landscapes and ornamentation. His beautifully engraved portraits, particularly those of King George V, King Edward VIII (55) and King George VI, are superb and, whilst different people will have their favourite example of his portraiture

55 Die proof of the head of King Edward VIII.

56 Griqualand revenue stamp.

work, the portrait of King George V in admiral's uniform, which was engraved for Rhodesian revenue stamps, must rate high on the list. His early work for the Royal Mint in 1910 produced the stamps based on the photograph of King George V by Downey, and in 1912 he produced the dies for the new portrait of the king which was taken from the head sculpted by Bertram Mackennal for use on coins and medals.

Harrison also produced the dies for the 1924/25 Wembley Exhibition stamps and within these items is a remarkable group of three die proofs which show the progression of the re-engraving of the 1924 die to the 1925 (**54**).

Colonial revenue stamps

Whilst the revenue issues of Great Britain appear in vast numbers in the Inland Revenue archive and the HMSO Collection, the colonial issues are not ignored, for these are to be found in the Kay Fiscal Collection of British Colonial revenue stamps, which covers a period up to about 1940.

The collection is very extensive and includes many rare and little-known issues, such as those produced for Griqualand (**56**) and the ranges of material used by the railways of the various Australian states, as well as a wide variety of excise revenue stamps.

Dr Edward Mosely

Another of the major collections of the British Library is that formed by Dr Edward Mosely, which was presented to the British Museum by his daughter in 1946. It is a collection devoted to the issues of British Africa and covers the period up to 1935. It principally contains unused material and there are very many rare items, particularly in the sections of the Cape of Good Hope, which includes an example of the extremely rare 1855–58 4d black (57) as well as examples of the previously described 'Woodblock' errors of colour.

There are fine ranges of the early issues of Mauritius, as well as a large range of the 1910–1916 double portrait issues of Rhodesia and the highly popular 1913–1922 issues which carry the portrait of King George V in full admiral's uniform.

The collections described in this book represent but a sample of the great wealth of philatelic collections which are now maintained at the British Library; they are arguably the finest philatelic collections in the world and, with their continued growth, provide a major legacy for generations to come.

57 Cape of Good Hope 1855–58 4d black.

58 Natal 1859–62 die proofs.

Suggestions for further reading

ROSSITER, STUART and FLOWER, JOHN, *The Stamp Atlas*, Macdonald & Co. (Publishers) Ltd., London 1986

WATSON, JAMES, *The Stanley Gibbons Book of Stamps and Stamp Collecting*, Windward, Leicester, 1981

WILLIAMS L. N. and M., *Fundamentals of Philately*, American Philatelic Society, State College, Pennsylvania, 1971

WILLIAMS, L. N. and M., *The Postage Stamp. Its History and Recognition*, Penguin, London, 1956

WILLIAMS, L. N. and M., *Rare Stamps*, George Weidenfeld and Nicolson Ltd., London, 1967

WILLIAMS, L. N. and M., *Stamps of Fame*, Blandford Press, London, 1949

WILLIAMS, L. N., *Encyclopedia of Rare and Famous Stamps*, Habsburg, Feldman S.A., Geneva, forthcoming 1988

The British Library Philatelic Collections are accessible to both the general visitor and serious student alike. More than sixty thousand items are displayed on six thousand leaves in cases in the British Library's public galleries. Facilities are provided for students to have access by prior appointment to any of the material within the Collections and full information respecting access is given in the information leaflet published by the British Library Philatelic Collections.